RAINY RIVER GIRL

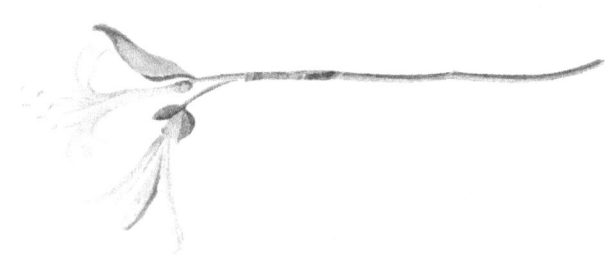

A MEMOIR

TOBY M. GERSHFIELD
and
JAMES N. GERSHFIELD

Scribal
Scion
Publishing

Rainy River Girl: A Memoir

Toby M. Gershfield and James N. Gershfield

Illustrations by James N. Gershfield

Cover design by Olivia M. Hammerman

ISBN-13: 979-8-88665-010-5, Paperback
ISBN-13: 979-8-88665-011-2, Hardcover

Published by Scribal Scion Publishing
Teaneck NJ, USA

Library of Congress Control Number: 2024939747

First Edition, published in 2024

Scribal Scion Publishing is an imprint of
Scribal Scion Publishing LLC

https://scribalscionpublishing.com

Other books by James N. Gershfield:
The Illuminated Omer Counting Book
The Illuminated Omer Counting Book Sephardic Edition

Dedication

Despite extreme challenges encountered by immigrants in general, our parents not only overcame unique and personal challenges, but also and importantly, excelled at honoring their parents and bringing new life to our extended Helman family. Indeed, several generations can now look back with extreme pride and gratitude for the sacrifices made. I certainly know what my father Frank (Ephraim) and my mother Lily (Leah Hindah) sacrificed to allow my sister and me to have the many opportunities and reasons to love them and our expanded families. We are proud of our Helman Family heritage, and our extended family in every way.

Sandy Helman

Acknowledgements

The authors thank the following people for their kind support of the publication of this book:

Paula Throckmorton
Frank Lozada
Rabbi Shawn B. Zell
Anonymous

Contents

Part One

Rainy River Prelude

What's a Dentist?

It was a cold, windy, and snowy, winter day in Winnipeg, Manitoba, in the early 1930's. And when I say cold and windy, I mean "rub the skin off your face if you don't have a scarf wrapped around your head" cold and windy. The snow in Winnipeg is very dry and gritty, like sand, and when it hits your face at 40 degrees below zero Fahrenheit, which by the way is the same as 40 below zero Centigrade, if your face isn't wrapped in something like a heavy wool scarf, you WILL lose facial skin.

Nothing very unusual as far as the weather was concerned, but it was a special day for another reason. It was a day that started a sequence of events that would change my life significantly as a little Jewish girl and how I viewed the world that I lived in.

My parents had been married for a couple of years and were talking about making plans for the future. I hadn't been born yet, so they were still living the life of a young couple with no kids.

And in those days, there was an expectation for young Jewish couples to start building a family soon after getting married.

My mother, Sophie, told my father "You know, Nathan, you don't have a good paying job. You can quote Shakespeare from memory, which is one of the things I love about you and attracted me to you when I first met you." You see, my parents had met on a blind date in a library in Winnipeg, and they discovered that they were both avid readers of Shakespeare. It was love at first verse, so to speak. "But that won't put food on the table and pay for all our other expenses. You need to do something to earn a decent living. Especially if we want to start a family."

"Well," said my father in a small, gentle voice, as he typically did, "what should I do? I don't have any skills that people will pay me much money for. I was working as an operator of a pants pressing machine until very recently, but my flat feet hurt so much after standing all day in front of the pants press that I had to quit that job." The pants press was a large machine that you had to stand in front of, and you would pull the upper part down onto the pants, and it would press a whole pair of pants in one motion. "What else can I do?", asked my father.

My mother thought about it for a minute, and then responded, "Why don't you become a dentist?" "A dentist? What's a dentist?", my father inquired softly. "A dentist is someone who takes care of people's teeth", my mother explained. "Oh, I didn't know that. We didn't have any dentists in Zelva. If someone had a sore tooth and needed it pulled out, we would just tie a string between the tooth and a doorknob, and quickly shut the door. And then, no more tooth!"

Zelva was the name of the little town in Lithuania where my father had lived as a young man before moving with his parents to Canada in the 1920's. He had worked as a clerk in the Zelva post office, so at least he knew how to handle the mail. When he first came to Canada from Zelva with his parents, as a young man, they were given a few acres of land and a horse by the government to create a home. They had to build a house by hand, and they worked the land as farmers. So he also learned something about farming and growing plants. But growing vegetables wasn't a viable career in the city of Winnipeg.

One of my father's strengths was his resolve to improve himself. When newcomers came to Canada, many of them would work during the day and take special English classes at night, so that they could become productive members of society. My father decided that he wanted to learn even more about many things, not just how to speak English, and the evening classes just did not provide enough of an education. So he went to public elementary school as a teenager and sat with the little children in the classroom in order to learn English. I'm sure the little kids thought that it was very funny seeing a person several years older than them squeezed into a little children's chair and trying to learn the basics of English and other subjects.

When we are children it's easier to learn a new foreign language, but when you get older it becomes much harder. My father was very determined, and he put a lot of effort into his elementary school studies. The results of his efforts were that he moved up through the grades quickly. But he didn't learn anything about medicine or dentistry in the public elementary school. And he needed to learn about those things in order to become a practicing dentist.

"How can I learn to be a dentist?", he asked. My mother thought again carefully for another minute or two, and had the answer: "There is a dental school in Toronto. You could go there and learn dentistry". It sounded like a good idea to my father. At least he didn't see anything wrong with the idea, and it sounded a lot better than standing all day in front of a hot pants press. And he figured that the chairs in the dental school classrooms would be larger than the little chairs he had to squeeze himself into in elementary school. So my father enrolled in the dental school, and off to Toronto they went.

Hello Canada

While my father was studying dentistry in Toronto, I was born. But I wasn't born in Toronto. As I recall, there wasn't a hospital in Toronto at that time that was recommended highly enough as a place to give birth for my parents to want to go there. As a result, my mother went to the Winnipeg General Hospital, in Winnipeg Manitoba, to bring me into the world. Apparently that hospital had a better reputation as a birthing hospital, and my parents felt more comfortable using that one. And my mother's timing was good. I was born in the summertime, after the snows had melted in the Southern part of Canada, so the travel was easier between Toronto and Winnipeg.

The man that I would eventually marry, at age twenty, was born four days before me in the same hospital in Winnipeg. My late husband used to say that when he was in the baby room at that hospital, he looked around and noticed a cute Jewish girl in a baby bed nearby, and he made a mental note to keep her in mind for the future. I was that little baby girl.

Soon after my mother gave birth, we were back in Toronto with my father. Time passed quickly, and within a few years my father had graduated from dental school, and we had moved back to Winnipeg with my mother and me.

By now, it was the mid-1930's. I was a happy child, living comfortably in my surroundings in Winnipeg, Manitoba, Canada, and enjoying a peaceful life as a tender toddler. The Great Depression was in its early stages, and events in Germany were starting to pave the way for World War Two and the vast destruction of European Jewry. But I didn't have any clue what was going on around me outside of my own little world. And in fact, I really didn't need to know, since my parents took care of everything for me. You could say that I was living in my own little "bubble", and I didn't mind at all.

My parents were religious Jews who observed and celebrated the Jewish Sabbath and holidays. My mother would light the Sabbath candles on Friday evenings, and would serve gefilte fish for dinner. She used to make the gefilte fish herself by grinding raw fish using a hand grinder and then mixing it with seasonings and cooking it.

Winnipeg was, and still is, a city with a relatively large Jewish population. It had so many Jews that it became known as the Jerusalem of Canada. Similarly, in Lithuania, which had a large Jewish population before World War Two, the city of Vilna was known as the Jerusalem of Lithuania. My mother's father was a famous Rabbi in Canada, who was heavily involved in the larger Canadian Jewish community, not just Winnipeg. He eventually was given the official title Chief Rabbi of Western Canada. My mother took the Jewish religion to heart, and was very observant of Jewish religious practices. Living in a large Jewish community like Winnipeg, Manitoba made it relatively easy to do so. Everything was going smoothly, and each day seemed to flow calmly into the next. But then, one day, something happened. Things were about to change for us in a big way.

Goodbye Winnipeg

My father was ready for his first job as a dentist. Little did he know that being a dentist would mean standing on his feet for long periods of time, just like standing in front of a pants press. It was probably a good thing that my mother didn't mention that small point to him before he finished dental school, or he might have quit before getting his degree!

There was one major problem, however, and I don't mean my father's flat feet. Who was going to hire a brand-new dentist who had just graduated from dental school, and had no experience? The demand for new dentists in Winnipeg was not very great. After doing some research, my parents learned about an opportunity for a dentist in a small town in rural Canada called Rainy River, Ontario.

There were no dentists at that time in Rainy River, so competition was non-existent. "Well", said my father quietly, "I suppose I could set myself up as the dentist of Rainy River to make a living, especially since there are no other dentists there. But we'll have to move to Rainy River and leave Winnipeg, although Rainy River is about 170 miles from Winnipeg so we could come back and visit every now and then by train without too much difficulty. There doesn't seem to be any Jewish community there, not even one synagogue, and no Jewish school for our daughter to attend and learn about her Judaism. Are you all right with that?" My mother replied, "Well, if that is what we need to do so that you can make a living and support our growing family, then that's fine with me."

So, off we went to Rainy River, Ontario, to start a new life, in a place that we knew almost nothing about. As it turned out, we would end up being the only Jewish family in town. In addition to there not being a synagogue, there was no Kosher butcher for buying Kosher meat, no Kosher restaurants for going out to eat, no Jewish schools, and no Jewish newspaper. There was basically nothing Jewish about the entire town. How would we be able to live there and fit in? It was certainly going to be a challenge and an adventure. I was only four years old at that time, but I remember those years very well.

Part Two

Hello Rainy River

The Town

The river which was known as the Rainy River lies on the border between the Province of Ontario in Canada and the State of Minnesota in the United States. When the white people came to Canada, the native peoples who lived there used to travel by river in canoes wherever they needed to go. There are many small rivers, called tributaries, in that area. The white people learned from the native peoples, and they followed the same small rivers to travel and to find food. Rainy River was not a very wide river, and you could easily see the land on the other side.

Perhaps not all roads, or rivers, lead to Rainy River, but in those days the railway lines did. The white people decided to build a railway in Canada, to make it easier to travel long distances. Remember, this was long before the airplane became a common way to travel in Canada. The train was a great invention that allowed people and goods to travel long distances, and in Canada there were some very long distances between cities and towns.

Canada is a very big country, about the same total square miles as the United States, and is still very underpopulated for its size, so you can imagine how sparsely populated it was back in the 1930's. Because of the relatively small population, the railroad ran through a lot of areas where there were no people at all – just land, trees, and animals. There weren't even many native people living in any one area. This was partly due to the fact that they tended to move around a lot, and didn't live for a long time in any one area.

As the seasons changed, the native peoples would move from one place to another primarily to find new food sources. The white people who moved into the areas where the natives lived built houses and created permanent settlements. There was a lot of wood in the forests, so the white people cut down many trees and built numerous houses out of the wood they got from the trees.

Trains are mechanical devices, and like all mechanical devices they needed servicing at regular intervals. To accomplish this, the Canadian Pacific Railway built several towns along the rail lines to service the trains. That is how and why the small town called Rainy River was originally created. Just for the sake of clarity, for the rest of this book, the words Rainy River will refer to the town and not to the river itself.

Rainy River was built very close to the river, and was situated between the river and the railroad, which was just North of the town. The entire town was only a few blocks in either direction. When I was there, the population was about 1,000 people. It doesn't seem like much has changed in that regard, because recent population estimates in the year 2022 are about the same.

You might be wondering how I know so much about the history of Canada. Well, I used to spend a lot of my time reading many books. There was no television, no Internet, and certainly no cell phones to distract me from reading books. I didn't like to fish, or go hiking, or do much of anything really, other than read books. The main way that I learned about Canada, its people and history was by spending time reading. Now that I am much, much older, I still like to read books rather than watch television or browse the Internet.

Rainy River gets hot in the summer, and cold and snowy in the winter. There is enough rain in the spring and summer so that the grass is very green, and the trees are full of leaves. Everything seems to grow very well. Not what you might expect from a country that is known for lots of snow and ice. Perhaps this is because there is a river nearby.

Due to the river, the water level in the ground is high. When I lived in Rainy River, there was a mixture of houses with and without basements. The house that we lived in had a basement.

Family Roots

Before I start telling you about my adventures in the town, I want to give you a little background about my parents. My mother was born in Europe in Suvalk, Lithuania around the year 1900. There were regular "pogroms", or attacks on Jews, in that area, and life was not easy if you were Jewish. Lithuania was an area where a lot of Jews lived in the early 1900's.

My father was from a different town in Lithuania, called Zelva. He was born sometime in the winter, but the exact year is not known. We believe that he was born between 1904 and 1907, but the exact year is unclear. He claimed that the town records in Zelva were burned during World War One. Soldiers came from both sides, and there was a lot of fighting, and many people were killed. Many historical records in Zelva were destroyed. My father never really talked about himself very much, so I wasn't sure what he was interested in doing. Now that I think of it, he didn't talk much in general and was a relatively quiet person.

Zelva was a town with a majority of people who were Jewish. It was actually a relatively important town for the Jews of Europe because it was one of the towns where the Rabbis of Lithuania came together every few years at the Zelva town fair, and discussed any Jewish legal problems that needed to be resolved.

My father's parents had inherited a big house in Zelva which they shared with another family of other relatives. That area of Zelva was originally in Lithuania, but it eventually became part of Poland, Russia, and Germany, depending on what was happening at any given time.

A Quick Tour

L et me give you a little "tour" of the small town of Rainy River, as I recall it. The main street was where the bakeries were and a very old house that was close to the river. Further away from the river, there was a drug store at the corner of that block, and my father's dental office was on the second floor above the drug store.

Across the street from the drug store was a store with big tables in it, but I'm not sure what kind of store it was. I remember seeing one item in that store – a tall pair of rubber wading boots that go way up your legs for standing in the river when you go fishing.

Almost all the buildings in Rainy River were very low, only one story high. One of the few exceptions was the building that my father's dental office was in. That building was a two story "skyscraper". I remember having to walk up the steps to get to the second floor where the dental office was. The single drug store in town was on the first floor of that building.

Looking North from there, you would see the railway line running from East to West. There was a small building where you could buy train tickets, and there was a wooden platform made from slats of wood.

When we travelled every now and then from Rainy River to Winnipeg, the train would stop in Rainy River in the middle of the night, at 2:30 AM. I remember standing on the platform with my mother late at night waiting for the train to come to take us back to Winnipeg. Amazingly, I felt safe standing there. When I was with my parents, I would not worry about anything. Luckily, nothing bad ever happened while waiting for the train in the early hours of the morning.

The Railroad

Most of the people who lived in Rainy River worked for the railroad, and that was the primary reason, and for some, the only reason, why they were there. There were also people there whose main purpose was to service the railroad workers.

The town had one doctor, one dentist, one general store, one bakery for baking bread, and another smaller bakery for baking small cakes. Imagine that! In the tiny town of Rainy River there were two bakeries. That might have been the only thing that Rainy River had two of at that time.

There was also a shoemaker shop. I went into the shoemaker shop once because a daughter of the owner was a classmate of mine and she invited me into their house, which served as their store.

At some point, it was pointed out to me that there was a large building on the other side of the tracks. That building was for the workers to fix railway cars, a "roundhouse" as they called it. Tracks came into the building from various directions, and a section of track was on a sort of turntable that could turn around with a railroad car on it, so the car could face another direction.

I remember seeing one of those small, manually operated rail cars that a worker could stand on and pump the handle up and down to make the car go. You can find those kinds of manually operated vehicles now in railroad museums.

I heard that the oatmeal porridge on the train was much softer and tastier than the porridge we had at home in Winnipeg. For those of you who don't know what porridge is, it's sort of like cooked oatmeal cereal, and that's what we called it back then. But, from what I heard at the time, the porridge on the train was made with cream instead of milk, and with added sugar. In Winnipeg we never added sugar to the oatmeal, probably because we couldn't afford the cost of sugar during the Great Depression. Apparently, they served very fancy porridge on the train!

I don't remember ever seeing a whole train while I was in Rainy River, so I don't know whether they had a caboose. They probably had them, I just can't remember. But I do remember being helped up the steps into the train car, because the steps were very high. At least they seemed very high to little me.

Inside the train cars, there were benches rather than individual seats, with an aisle down the middle. The benches were situated back-to-back, so when you sat on one of the benches you were facing people sitting on an opposing bench.

The trains ran in the middle of the night, and my mother used to tell me to lie down on the bench and try to go to sleep. I would sing quietly to myself, and my voice would sound funny because of the bumpy motion of the train. It was difficult to fall asleep while on the train. Little babies seemed to enjoy the motion of the train and it helped them to fall asleep. But I wasn't a baby anymore - I was already a young girl.

The Theater

One of the first things that we did after we moved to Rainy River was to attend a live play that was performed in a large building within the town. At least the building seemed big to me at the time because I was so small. It must have been shortly after we arrived in the summer, and I had just turned five years old.

I remember sitting in the audience with my mother and father. The play was on an elevated stage. The actors were talking, and at one point in the play they opened a trunk. Someone got into it and pulled a cover over themselves in order to hide. Then someone else came onto the stage and asked where that person was. I was just a little kid who didn't know any better, and I yelled out "He's in the trunk!" Everyone started laughing. I was very embarrassed about the whole thing. I realized later that the audience was not supposed to say anything during a play. But how was I supposed to know? There weren't any announcements before the play started about not saying anything during the play.

They also used to show movies in that building, and the stage had some type of screen for showing the movies. When I started going to school, I found out that they showed little movies for children on Saturdays. The only one I can remember was called Captain Marvel – a short movie about a flying ship that could fly in outer space. My mother bought tickets ahead of time, so that the tickets would not need to be bought on Shabbat, the Jewish Sabbath. The equipment that they showed in the film next to the human actors was drawn by hand by special movie artists. The level of sophistication in movie special effects was rather crude at that time, compared to what can be done now using high powered computer graphics software.

Up to My Neck in Snow

One of the very fun things that I used to do together with the other kids in town during the winter was to play in the snow. There were drainage ditches next to the roads in those days, and they didn't yet have storm sewer pipes underneath the streets. Whenever it snowed, the snow would accumulate in the drainage ditches, and eventually there would be a couple of feet of snow in them. I was only around two years old when we moved to Rainy River, so I was very short, maybe just a little taller than the depth of the drainage ditches.

I had a very good snow suit that my parents gave me, and it kept me very warm and comfortable in the snow. So, what we kids used to like to do was to bury ourselves in the snow up to our necks, so that only our heads were visible. I suppose this is similar to the way that some kids bury themselves in the sand at the beach during the summer, except that this was in the snow in the middle of the winter.

One day, after we had buried ourselves in the snow, and I was very relaxed and enjoying the experience, I realized that all of the other kids had left, probably to go back home to their parents, and I was left all alone buried in the snow up to my neck. For some reason, I didn't feel the urge to go back home, and I was enjoying just staying there and watching what was going on around me. The snow suit kept me so warm and comfortable that I just stood there quietly surrounded by the snow. Even if I had wanted to go home, I didn't know how to get myself out of the snow by myself, so I was stuck there until someone would come by and help me.

Eventually, my mother started worrying about where I was because I hadn't come home around the time that I usually did. She started calling all of the neighbors asking them whether anyone had seen me, and they all said that they didn't know where I was.

My mother was really getting worried after that, and she decided to go outside and search for me. I saw her walking around looking for me, but I was so happy and comfortable in my snowy cocoon that I didn't think to call out to her. I just stayed quietly in the snow. Finally, my mother noticed a small head sticking up out of the snow at the side of the road, and realized that it was my head! She helped pull me out of the snow and we went home together.

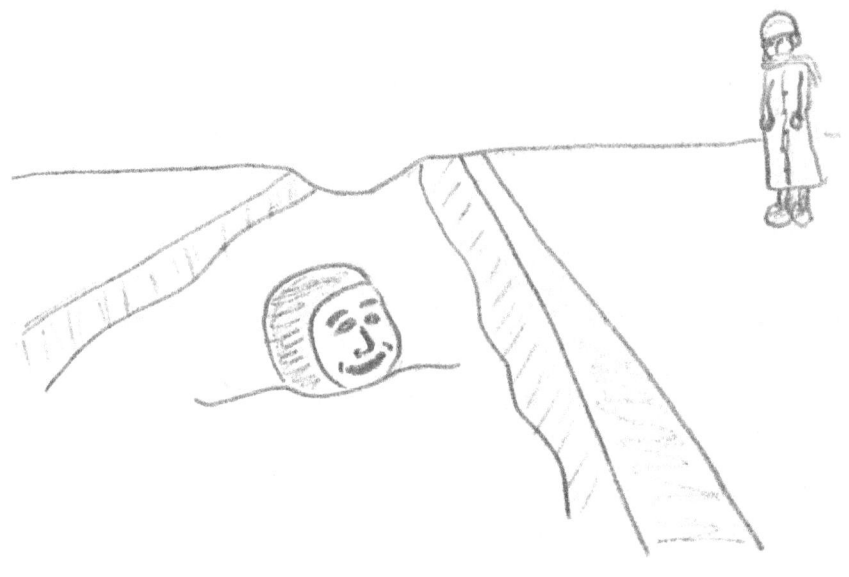

The Dental Office

My father's dental office consisted of a few rooms. It had a waiting room with a few chairs in it, another room with the dental chair and equipment for drilling teeth, and a third room for other equipment and tools that a dentist needs. In the room with the electric dental chair that my father used regularly, there was an antique dental chair that didn't use electricity to move it up and down or to tilt the seat back. Instead, there was foot pedal that you would step on to make the chair move up and down using hydraulic pressure.

In those days, dentists used mercury to make fillings for cavities in teeth. I remember seeing my father mixing the materials for fillings. The mercury that he used was like little balls, and it would roll away easily. It was a lot of work to mix the mercury with the other ingredients that you had to use in order to make the material that could be put into a tooth cavity. I suppose the dentists of that time didn't realize that mercury was an unhealthy substance to put into someone's mouth, but they didn't have anything better to use.

In the waiting room, there was a potbelly stove in the middle of the room. It had a flat top and was the size of a small child. It had a little door in it for putting wood in. The door was made from metal, and it had a little window in it made from mica, a kind of translucent stone. When the fire was burning inside the stove, the mica would display different colors, like yellow and gold. It was very pretty to look at when the fire was burning. But in the summer, when the fire was not lit, it just looked dark brown.

There was also a very nice mirror on one of the walls in the waiting room. It was about six inches high and perhaps three feet wide. The center part was a regular mirror that you could use to look at yourself. The two side parts had a beautiful landscape picture painted on them. I had never seen something like that before. It was very unusual, and I enjoyed looking at the pictures whenever I was in the waiting room.

The waiting room had a window facing the main street. To get to the waiting room, first you had to enter the drug store, and then you had to open a door to the staircase that went up to the waiting room. Once you were inside that room, you could see a door that opened into the dental office, which also had windows facing the main street.

Our House

For $25 per month, my father paid rent for a two-story house and the dental office that was above the drug store. The house must have made a very strong impression on me as a child because when I have trouble sleeping, I close my eyes and visualize walking around the house. Thinking about that house makes me feel comfortable and helps me feel relaxed.

Let me start by describing the outside of the house. If you approached the house from the railroad, which wasn't that far away, there was a public sidewalk for about a block and a half. Then, you made a right turn onto a sidewalk that was inside the yard.

The first thing you saw at that point was a beautiful honeysuckle bush. I remember being small enough to fit inside that bush. I used to like crawling into it and having the branches surround me. There were nice smelling flowers inside the honeysuckle bush. It was my little hiding place, where I could escape from the world and feel safe and sound.

Another thing that I liked in the front yard was a small tree stump. It was a bit too high for me, but with a little effort I was able to get myself up onto it and sit on it. This would be a nice place to sit and watch the scenery. My mother was always suggesting that I go outside and get some fresh air. I figured that I could sit on the tree stump if I had nothing else to do, and then my mother would be happy.

The yard was actually a double yard. The houses in Rainy River were built close together, but for some reason this house had a large yard with a lot of grass. If you walked toward the house, you would see a big porch with screening on it to keep out the bugs. In front of the porch were nasturtium flowers. They were a beautiful mixture of colors: yellow, red, and orange. I've always loved flowers, and especially yellow and red flowers.

If you walked around the house to the left, there was English Ivy growing with very big leaves, on the South corner, so it got a lot of sun in the morning. There wasn't any house right next to it to provide any shade, but the leaves of the ivy were so large that it shaded the porch. It was shady and cool on the porch in the summer because of the ivy.

Then, if you walked along the side of the house, there were nice blue flowers, which I think were Morning Glory flowers. They also got the full sun, which made them grow very well. Walking toward the back of the yard, asparagus used to come up from the ground in the springtime. I remember that it grew very quickly. Even from one day to the next, you could tell that it had grown bigger.

I was told that you shouldn't pull asparagus out of the ground because that would disturb the roots. Instead, you should cut it with a knife and then cook it and eat it. One of the reasons why I have always liked to eat asparagus is because it reminds me of Rainy River.

The asparagus didn't grow for very long. It came up in the spring, we harvested it, and then it stopped growing. And then, later in the summer, there were pretty little white flowers called Baby's Breath that grew in the same place. At the time, I used to wonder whether these flowers had any relationship with the asparagus. But, of course, they didn't since it was its own kind of plant.

I remember seeing clotheslines where my mother would hang up the wash to dry in the sunlight. At our house in Winnipeg, where we lived after moving from Rainy River, we also had clotheslines in the back yard.

There was a large barn near the house, and my father used to tell me not to go in there because items might fall on me. He didn't say exactly what might fall on me. Was it the barn door, or something else? What could possibly fall on me inside a barn? The person who delivered the wood for the winter used to leave it piled up on the outside of the barn, so it wasn't going to fall on me inside the barn. The main message was clear, however: "Don't go into the barn". So, I didn't.

Next to the barn was a great big pile of cut wood that my father needed to chop with an axe because there was a wood burning stove in the kitchen, and the stove needed small bits of wood to make heat and for cooking. The stove had legs and that allowed air to pass underneath it.

The house did not have hot running water. We only drank hot

tea, and no coffee. For many years afterwards, I and my husband would mainly drink tea whenever we wanted a hot drink. If you wanted a hot cup of tea you had to make sure that there was a fire going in the stove so you could heat the water. If you wanted to wash the dishes, you needed to heat the water on the stove. Also, if you wanted a hot bath, you needed to heat up water on the stove. I remember my mother walking up the stairs to a second floor bathroom that had a big bathtub, carrying hot water up the stairs from the stove to pour into the bathtub. Without that wood burning stove, life would have been a lot different. Who knows whether we could have survived without that stove.

I don't recall how my mother washed our clothes. We didn't have a clothes washing machine, so she must have done it all by hand somehow. In general, I don't know how a lot of things were done by my mother because I didn't pay attention to what my mother did most of the time. My mother would tell me frequently to just go outside and play with the other kids. So, I did.

In Rainy River, crime was not a major problem. I remember that our front door was never locked, and I never had to carry a key with me. I just went in and out whenever I felt like it.

When I was eight years old, my father tried to teach me how to chop wood with the axe. Knowing how to chop firewood was an important skill in those days. But when my mother saw what he was trying to do, she forbade me from chopping wood because of the danger. So, I never got a chance to chop wood. It wasn't a great loss, however. Right after marrying my husband, the one who saw me when we were both babies in the hospital, we moved to Manhattan where we didn't need to chop wood. I don't recall seeing anyone chopping wood in Manhattan. And I never developed a desire to be a lumberjack either, even though I grew up in Canada.

In the front of our house there was a short sidewalk that led from the street to the house through the front yard, and then there were four steps to get up to the porch. There was a screen door that you had to open at the top of the steps because the whole porch was enclosed with screening. I remember that there were many flies in Rainy River in the summertime. Very large black flies. Oddly enough, there were no mosquitoes, as I recall. Just gigantic black flies.

Then there was a wooden door that led into the house. When you entered the house, in front of you there were steps leading up to the second floor. There was a door on the left to the living room. On the right was a large foyer area. If you walked straight ahead, you would get to the kitchen, which is where I spent most of my time because it was the warmest part of the house.

The kitchen had a large black iron stove that burned wood inside. It had a small oven built into it. And on top it was all flat, and there were no burners. Just round metal disks. You had to use a special tool to lift up each of the disks, so that you could poke at the burning wood to push it around. As a little kid, I had nothing to do with that, but I remember my mother doing that.

Next to the stove, on the left side, there was a big sink. I remember once seeing fish swimming in the sink in some water. You see, my mother made her own gefilte fish from scratch, and she used a hand grinder to grind the fish. You can't get fresher gefilte fish than hand grinding fish which are swimming around in your kitchen sink!

The word "gefilte" is a Yiddish word that means "filled" or "stuffed", and it's called gefilte fish because originally gefilte fish was made by grinding fish meat and then putting it back inside the skin of the fish. But that was a very long time ago.

To the left of the main staircase of the house, past the door to the living room, was a door to the dining room which was a very big room. On the left-hand side of the kitchen was the sink, a door that connected to the dining room and a storage unit (like a tall cabinet).

The storage unit had a pull-out bin with a handle for keeping flour in it. You see, in those days most people did a lot of their own baking. They would get a big sack of flour and put the flour in the bin. One day, my mother opened the flour bin, and a mouse jumped out! I was sitting at the kitchen table, and it was kind of scary.

The dining room was a large room, and it had a very nice window in it facing South. It was a three part window shaped like a letter U, kind of like a bay window. If you made a left turn in the dining room you would be facing the living room. There must have been a door between the rooms, because in the winter when it was cold they brought beds down and everyone slept in the dining room, because that room was kept warm by the heat coming from the stove in the kitchen.

The living room had a fireplace in it, but I don't remember it ever being used. It had a small desk, and windows facing the porch. That is where I used to sit when my father tried to teach me to read, write and speak Hebrew. I would see the other kids playing outside and I wanted to go outside and play with them. But my mother supported my father's desire to teach me Hebrew instead of me playing outside. As it turned out, my mother was very smart in doing so, because by the time I went to Winnipeg for a year at age seven, I was able to read Hebrew.

In order to give us something fun to do indoors, my mother put a ping pong set on the table in the dining room. It was a very big table, big enough to play ping pong on.

So Much to Learn

I remember that my mother kept trying to get me to learn various things when I was little. I know that she loved me, and she wanted me to develop in many ways. But sometimes I just didn't like doing whatever it was she wanted me to learn, and I kept finding creative ways of getting out of learning them.

One time, my mother had a lady come to our house and teach me physical exercises, including how to dance like Shirley Temple. Apparently my mother was obsessed with Shirley Temple. But I had not seen Shirley Temple in the movies, and in fact I had never seen anybody dancing at all. So, I had no idea who she was, why people liked her, or what I was supposed to do.

The dance teacher would say "put your foot this way" and "put your foot that way". And she wanted me to jump up and click my heels together in mid-air, but that was too hard to do. The lady was able to demonstrate how to do it. She told me to try doing it while holding onto a chair, and said that after I learned how to do it while holding onto the chair, then later I could try doing it without holding onto the chair. I tried it with the chair, but it was so difficult that I didn't even get to the point of trying to do it without the chair. I kept losing my balance and just stopped doing it. As I recall, this was something that was done in the movies at that time and a lot of people were trying to imitate that dance move. You almost never see anyone doing that anymore.

My mother also had a man come over to teach me how to paint. He brought over a painting that he had made, and it had lots of bushes and green things and looked very nice. So, I actually wanted to learn because I thought that his painting looked very beautiful.

But when he came over to our house, he started drawing stick figures on a piece of paper. Just straight lines, that were supposed to be very simple pictures of people. And I thought, "What does that have to do with the painting that he showed me?" Well, it had nothing to do with the painting that he had shown me before, and I didn't know a lot, but I knew that people don't look like little straight lines.

He wanted me to draw stick figures too, to copy what he did using a pencil. I thought that was just stupid, and I told my mother how ridiculous the drawings were. He never came again.

Then, my mother got a violin from Toronto, and there was a nice lady in Rainy River who came over to teach me how to play. The teacher told me what to do, but it made terrible sounds. My mother would be in the kitchen, and I would be in the dining room. My mother remembers hearing me ask the lady a question, where to put my fingers. The lady never answered. So my mother figured that the lady was hard of hearing. I was about five years old at the time, and the teacher was younger than my mother, maybe in her 20's.

I remember lying in bed and thinking that the "music" that was coming out of the violin sounded terrible. So, one day I came down to the kitchen and told my mother that the violin was broken and therefore I couldn't play it anymore. It wasn't really broken, I just figured that if I said that it was broken then I wouldn't need to take violin lessons anymore. After that, no more violin lessons.

There was a large radio in the living room. An old fashioned one with long legs on it, like a piece of furniture. Sometimes the radio was turned on, and I used to hear piano playing and liked the way it sounded. Then, I found out that there was a lady living across the street who taught piano.

So, I told my mother that I wanted to learn how to play the piano. My mother, who seemed to always be interested in having me learn new things, was very excited that I expressed interest in learning something, and she arranged for the lady to come over to our house. The lady drew piano keys on a piece of cardboard since my family did not own a piano. The lady then told me what to do with my fingers and to practice moving my fingers on the piece of cardboard, as though it was a piano keyboard. Not very realistic, but close enough to a real piano keyboard to get started.

At least she didn't draw a stick figure of a person playing piano. That would have certainly resulted in the end of my piano lessons.

I remember going across the street and listening to the lady playing on her piano. Eventually, my mother rented a piano from Toronto and I started taking lessons in our house. I can't remember which room the piano was in. When I went to Winnipeg for one year, I continued playing the piano. I started at age six in Rainy River, then one year in Winnipeg, and then again at age eight in Rainy River. I got pretty good at playing piano, and kept playing for many years after we moved to New York City.

When the piano lady invited me to her house, she pointed out some nice flowers growing in the front yard. The flowers were called snapdragons. When you pinched a snapdragon flower, which seem to have two main parts like a head and stomach, it would "open up". The head would go back, and the stomach would go down. The yard at that house was the only place I ever saw snapdragons.

A lot of the other places that my family lived in Winnipeg never had flowers around them. The flowers in Rainy River were very impressive. After we left Rainy River I always liked seeing flowers, whether they were real flowers or just flower patterns on our dishes and on my clothing.

The living room in our house was dark because of the porch in front of it, and the giant leaves of the ivy plants which provided a lot of shade. But the dining room was very bright because of the bay window. To save money, we never used the electric lights during the daytime, and kept them off as much as possible. We ended up staying out of the living room most of the time because it was so dark. Another reason we stayed out of the living room was that there was no furniture in that room and, it wasn't comfortable to sit on the hard wood floor.

Upstairs there was a room in front of the house. A big room with big windows, so it was very bright, but again no furniture. Furniture must have been too expensive for my parents to afford at that point in their lives. The room had a small walk-in closet, and there was another very small room in front of the closet with windows. I used to wonder what that other tiny room was for. Maybe it was designed to put a crib for a baby. It wasn't much bigger than that.

There were two other bedrooms, one for me and one for my parents. The other room that was above the dining room also had a bay window. And it attracted pigeons. They used to like to sit on the outside of the house and make their little pigeon sounds, what I like to call burbling noises. I used to like going into that room to listen to the pigeons and their funny noises.

Apparently, however, the neighbors didn't like pigeons, in spite of their interesting bird noises. My family was told one day to get out of the house because some people were going to come over to shoot the pigeons. I guess they really didn't like the noises that the pigeons made. We complied with the request since we didn't want to get shot accidentally. I never saw, or heard, any more pigeons at our house after that.

School Days

When I went to school, there were two different buildings. In Ontario, school started at age five. There was a house, just an ordinary looking house, with a yard in front and grass on the sides for grades one and two. During recess the students could go out and play or do whatever they wanted to do on the grass.

There was a separate building, for grades three and above. The reason for two school buildings was in order to keep the older school kids away from the younger five and six year olds, so that they would not hurt them.

There was one teacher for grades one and two. Grade one children sat on the left side of a big room, and grade two children sat on the right side. There were not that many children all together, just two or three rows of desks for each class. I can't remember exactly how many children sat in each row, but it couldn't have been that many.

I missed out on being in that first school building because I was kept out of school when I was five years old. Apparently, there was a problem with the water supply in town that year. It had gotten contaminated somehow, and there was a risk of people getting typhoid fever from drinking the water, so my mother kept me home for the whole school year so that I would avoid getting sick.

I remember a number of adults talking about keeping their newborn children in one of the drawers of their chest of drawers. This was related to the problem that caused the water to be contaminated. I'm not sure how keeping your baby in a drawer would keep it safe or healthier than not in a drawer. But a number of people thought it was a good idea. Maybe there was a fire, or maybe a flood, which caused contamination of the water and air. I don't remember exactly. Something happened, and there was a fear of sickness, and people did the best they could at the time with the tools that they had available.

During the year that I was kept at home, my mother started teaching me how to read English. By the time I turned six, and started attending the school, I knew how to read. But the teacher initially put me in the grade one section. After a while she realized that I knew how to read, and at that point I was moved from the grade one side to the grade two side of the room.

At the same time, while I was kept out of school, my father was teaching me how to read Hebrew. My parents sent me to Winnipeg for grade three, and I already knew how to read Hebrew by that time. When I was eight years old, my parents were still living in Rainy River, but I had moved to Winnipeg to stay with my maternal grandfather, Rabbi Israel Kahanovitch, so that I could get a solid Jewish education in Winnipeg.

My parents felt that it was important that I learn about my Jewish heritage, and unfortunately in Rainy River there were no Jewish schools at that time. My mother brought me back to Rainy River for grade four, and I continued my studies in that other building which was for the older students.

During recess time at the school, some boys would shout at another little boy, and I didn't like that. His name was Adolph and they called him "Hitler, Hitler" to make fun of him. Sometimes people don't really understand what they are saying, or how hurtful it can be. Years later, I reflected on that scene and made sense of it, and realized how horrible a thing it was to do to a fellow classmate. But at that time I didn't understand what the boys meant and why they were saying that. I just knew that it wasn't nice that they were making fun of him, and I felt bad for him.

Birthday Parties

For the first couple of years when we were living in Rainy River, I was invited to the birthday parties of the other children in town. At one party, I noticed that the metal stove in the kitchen had a large exhaust pipe that went up, but it didn't go through the ceiling the way those pipes usually do. Instead, it made a right turn before reaching the ceiling, and it went through the wall into the living room. Then it travelled for a while in the living room before making another turn and going up through the living room ceiling. I assume that the reason for this was to provide an extra source of heat in the winter.

At another birthday party, the family brought out a large serving dish with a large mound of something that kept wiggling and moving. It looked very strange, and I was afraid to even try eating any of it. Later I found out that it was a type of gelatin dessert, and the other girls liked to eat it.

When I was at my maternal grandfather's house in Winnipeg, they used to serve a Kosher version of a gelatin based side dish called Ptcha. It was made from the gelatin that can be extracted from cow bones. It was firmer in texture than the dessert I remember seeing at birthday parties in Rainy River. I wasn't a big fan of anything that wobbled on my plate, preferring to eat food that doesn't try doing a dance while I am looking at it, even though I enjoy watching ballet, so I stayed away from Ptcha and from any other gelatin desserts.

Part Three

A Winnipeg Interlude

Elementary School and the Talmud Torah

The year was 1940, and I was seven years old. My parents figured that it wasn't very good for my Jewish development to be in a town where we were the only Jewish family, so they sent me to Winnipeg to spend a year going to a Jewish school and learning more about my Jewish heritage. While I was in Winnipeg for that year, I lived with my maternal grandfather, Rabbi Israel Kahanovitch. I will have more to say about him a little bit later.

My mother thought that I knew enough to go into grade four. But when I arrived in Winnipeg and started to attend the public elementary school, the teacher didn't want to do that because then I would be two years younger than all the other students. So, I was put into grade three. The name of the school was the David Livingstone School, named after the famous explorer.

My Aunt Esther, one of my mother's sisters, was looking after me at my grandfather's house in Winnipeg. She was very busy teaching Kindergarten at the Talmud Torah school, which was a Jewish day school for children. My grandmother, Rabbi Kahanovitch's wife, had passed away in 1940. I remember seeing her when I was at their house attending the Passover Seder meals. One year at the Seder, there was a little old lady sitting next to my grandfather, but the next year she wasn't there. I couldn't figure out why she didn't want to attend the Seder. After all, it's one of the most important family events of the year for religious Jews. Many years later, I found a newspaper article that said that my grandmother had passed away that year, and that explained was why she was not there.

School hours were from 9 AM to 12 Noon. All students went home for lunch and had to be back in time for classes to start again at 1:30 PM. You see, the public schools did not serve lunch in those days. School ended every day at 4 PM. My maternal grandfather's house was right across the street from the school, which was very handy for me. There was no way I could get lost going home for lunch or going back to school after lunch. Even if there was a snowy blizzard, I didn't have very far to go.

The Jewish school, called the Talmud Torah, two Hebrew words that literally mean "Teaching Torah", was on Flora Avenue, in a building with beautiful grey stone on the outside. The younger children, I'm not sure of the exact age cutoff, went at 4:30 PM to the Talmud Torah, maybe for an hour or hour and a half, and then the older students went in.

When I was seven years old my class was only girls. We went to the Talmud Torah four days a week, Monday to Thursday, and also on Sunday mornings. There were enough students in the lower grades that the boys and girls could be split into separate classes, but not in the upper grades. It is the Jewish custom to separate boys and girls for religious studies so that the students can focus on their studies instead of focusing on each other.

My maternal grandfather died in 1945. I'm not sure whether he would have agreed to allow the boys and girls to study together in the same classroom after he was no longer with us.

Looking Smart

Sometimes it takes a while to understand what is going on around us. As an example, when I was in grade two back in Rainy River, we were given report cards to take home. At that time, I didn't understand the whole business of report cards, and I didn't know what their significance was. All I knew was that I had to take that thing called a report card back home from the school to my parents.

By the time I was seven years old, I finally became interested in looking at the report card and seeing what it was all about. After I read it, I realized that it was a fascinating thing containing subjects, numeric grades, and comments from teachers.

Unfortunately, my numbers were not very good, in the 50's. I had figured out by this time that 100 was the best, and I understood that 50 was not a good grade. I don't think that they graded on a "curve" as is done many times today, and I decided that I wanted to improve. I wanted to get better grades and determined that what I needed to do was to become "smart". I figured out that smart people got good grades, not realizing at that time that a large part of getting good grades was spending time and effort in studying and doing homework. But how was I going to become smart? I figured out a plan of attack.

I noticed that among the grown-ups, all the people who seemed to be smart wore glasses. So, I concluded from that observation that in order to become smart I also needed to wear glasses. I felt like I was starting to get smarter already, just thinking about it. But how was I going to get glasses?

I put my young brain to work, and I found a solution. I told my Aunt Esther, who was helping to take care of me in Winnipeg, that I had a hard time reading, and that I needed glasses. So, she took me to an eye doctor for an examination.

At the eye doctor, I realized that my eyesight was actually very good, and I didn't really need glasses. But I had convinced myself that I needed the glasses to become smart, so I pretended that I couldn't see clearly. When I was standing in front of the "letter chart", I said that I could only see the big letter "E" at the top of the chart, and that all of the other letters were out of focus.

This must have convinced the eye doctor that I needed glasses, and he prescribed glasses for me with circular lenses and wires going over my ears. In those days we called that style of glasses "granny glasses". I didn't care what the glasses looked like. All I cared about was getting glasses so that they would make me smart. And that's how I got eyeglasses.

After I got my glasses, I was so happy. I was going to become smart! Unfortunately, when I went to school in Winnipeg, the coat that I wore had no pockets, so I wasn't able to take my glasses with me to school. I didn't want to just carry them loose in my hands. I did have a little box that I carried to school every day, but it only had enough room to store the pencils that I had to take with me to class, so there was no room to put the glasses in it. After all of that work, I couldn't take my glasses with me to school. As it turned out, I was smart enough without the glasses, and I realized eventually that the glasses are not something that makes you smart.

Snip, Snip

While living in Winnipeg with my maternal grandfather, my Aunt Esther had to comb my hair in the morning. You see, my mother had been doing that in Rainy River and I didn't know how to get my own hair ready in the morning by myself. But Aunt Esther had trouble combing my hair, because it was rather long and would get all tangled up while I was sleeping at night. So, she decided to simplify things and cut off my hair. She cut it extremely short because she didn't have time to comb my hair in the morning.

My grandfather had a very big cat, with very long hair. Apparently my Aunt Esther didn't feel the need to cut the cat's hair very short. But it was probably a good thing that she didn't. The cat used to spend time outside the house in the winter in addition to inside the house, so the long hair helped to keep the cat warm.

When I was seven years old, I did what I was told. I hadn't developed the ability to say "no" to people older than me, and I certainly wasn't going to tell my Aunt Esther to not cut my hair.

My aunt started cutting my hair. When it was falling on the floor it scared the cat. Perhaps the cat thought that it was going to be the next in line to get a haircut. The hair had been growing since the time I was born, so there was a lot of it, and it was quite long.

Then my aunt decided to take me to a barber shop to "finish" the haircut. It was about a block and a half away, on Main Street near Flora Avenue. In the North part of Winnipeg, the main street was called Main Street. That sounded to me like a good name for a main street.

At the barber shop, I sat in a big barber chair and the barber snipped away. He gave me "bangs", which I had never had before. When I came back to Rainy River in the spring to visit during the Jewish holiday of Passover, my mother saw my new haircut. She was horrified by the strange way my hair looked. Not to mention the round granny glasses that she hadn't seen before. Oh my! I must have looked really strange to her.

You see, my mother was very proud of my hair. Shirley Temple was popular at the time, and my mother would try to make my hair look like Shirley Temple's curly hair. She would take a comb and wind my hair around a finger which would create a nice curl. She was very thrifty. Why buy curlers when you can use your fingers? Seeing my crazy looking haircut might have been what convinced my mother to move me back from Winnipeg to Rainy River!

My Grandfather the Chief Rabbi

My maternal grandfather, Rabbi Israel Kahanovitch, was born in Grodno, Poland. He studied to be a Rabbi at the Jewish schools, called Yeshivot, in Grodno and in Slobodka, which was a town in Lithuania. He was ordained as a Rabbi at a very young age, and he left Europe and traveled to North America soon after the Pogroms in the early 1900's. He spent his first year as the Rabbi of a congregation in Scranton, Pennsylvania, but moved to Canada the next year in 1907 and settled in Winnipeg, Manitoba.

Gradually, my maternal grandfather's reputation grew among the Jews in Manitoba and the provinces to the West, and he became the Chief Rabbi of Western Canada. He was honored as a National Historic Person in Canada by the Canadian government in 2016.

Part of his job was to organize the community and make sure that the Hebrew Schools were supervised properly. Another part of his job was to supervise Kashrut in Canada. He trained some men from Europe to be Kosher slaughterers. Winnipeg was a crossroads and a big town for handling cattle. The Jews in Winnipeg established Kosher facilities.

My mother explained once that when the animal was slaughtered, a stamp was put on it in purple ink, on the carcass after the skin was removed. According to Ashkenazic Jews the back end of the cow is not Kosher because of the sciatic nerve, so they would give the hind part of the animal to the non-Jews. But then the Jews could use the front part as long as it was stamped. That meant that the cow had been slaughtered using an extra sharp knife. To test the sharpness, you can use your tongue. Or you can use your thumb nail instead, if you don't want to risk cutting yourself. The thumb nail is surprisingly sensitive, and can detect very minor imperfections in a knife blade.

My mother told me that there was only one butcher shop in Winnipeg that followed her father's rules to the letter, and that was the only one that she dealt with. It was very close to the Talmud Torah building. I went in there when I was around 10 years old to see what it was like.

Rabbi Kahanovitch was very interested in keeping his body in good shape. He would exercise regularly. He set up a bar in one of the door frames in the house, and he would do chin up exercises.

He wasn't very tall or big, but he was trim and fit, which was unusual for a Rabbi. When you are a Rabbi, you need to sit and study for many hours each week, and there isn't a lot of time for physical exercise or going to the gym.

The Cat, the Chicks, and the Goat

Rabbi Kahanovitch had a house cat. I used to like watching it. It seemed to understand what my grandfather was saying to it, but he used to speak the Yiddish language in the house. The cat must have been smart enough to understand Yiddish. I remember suggesting to my grandparents that instead of washing the dishes by hand, they could just put them on the floor and let the cat lick them clean. It made sense to me, but they didn't like that idea and just kept washing the dishes the same old way.

The stove in the kitchen in Rabbi Kahanovitch's house had legs, just like the one in Rainy River. The legs were tall enough that there was space to put things underneath it and keep them warm. I remember seeing a box with baby chicks in it under the stove to keep them warm in the winter. They would have just frozen to death outside the house.

There came a time when Rabbi Kahanovitch was diagnosed with diabetes. The doctors told him that goat milk would be good for him and would help his diabetes. So, he asked his Shamos, known as a Sexton in English, the person at the synagogue who helps take care of the building, to go buy a goat at the farmers market which was held regularly near the house.

There was a big open space where the farmers came to sell things in the city, in stalls. And people from the city would come to buy things from the farmers. Doing as he was told, the Shamos went to the farmers market, bought a nice goat and brought it back.

Then Rabbi Kahanovitch looked over the goat and said to the Shamos, "That's a very fine goat that you purchased, but where am I supposed to get the milk from this goat?" Apparently, the Shamos has bought a male goat by mistake, perhaps not realizing that the purpose of the goat was to provide milk for Rabbi Kahanovitch. The Shamos had to go back and exchange the goat for a pregnant female goat.

Not long after that, the goat had two babies, one male and one female. The mother goat rejected the male baby and didn't let it get any milk. The goat would kick its baby if he tried getting close to drink milk. In order that the baby male goat wouldn't starve, I had to feed it myself.

I used to feed it milk out of a glass milk bottle with a nipple on the end. I did that early in the morning every day before going to school. I would sit on the back steps which were on the side of the house that led into the summer kitchen. I would hold the milk bottle up, and the goat would come walking up to the bottle. I had to hold onto the bottle with both hands so it wouldn't drop on the steps and break. The goat pulled very strongly on the bottle with its mouth, and I had to hold on tightly.

Fire! Fire!

One time when I was staying with my maternal grandfather in Winnipeg, I attended a special Hanukkah celebration at his synagogue. As I recall, there was a group of other Jewish girls there, including many of my friends. We were each given a stick with an apple at the top of the stick. Above each apple was a candle. At some point in the celebration, we each lit our own candle and started parading around the synagogue in a line while holding the sticks with the apples and burning candles in front of us.

One of the girls was walking a little too close behind me, and suddenly her candle caused my hair to catch on fire. I'm sure it caused quite a commotion. I don't remember how I survived that accident, but I did. Probably my long hair was at least partly to blame for the accident. After that event, my hair was cut short for the remainder of my stay in Winnipeg so that I would be safe.

Part Four

Hello Again Rainy River

Bigger and Better

After spending a year in Winnipeg, expanding my knowledge of the Jewish tradition, it was time to go back to Rainy River. One of the first things I did when we arrived in town was to run to the Honeysuckle bush, my favorite hiding place, and climb inside. I missed sitting inside the branches and flowers, and I was very excited to get back to a comforting place. But, when I tried to get inside the bush, I couldn't get in. I was too big! I had grown so much during the year in Winnipeg that I was too large to fit inside the bush. Now where could I go when I wanted to be alone and get away from the world? I needed to find a new hiding place, but it was going to be harder now that I had grown so much.

I also tried sitting on the tree stump that I used to sit on when I was told to go outside and play. But now the stump looked really tiny, and it was just too small for me to sit on it comfortably anymore. It also seemed to be much lower than it was before, and it seemed to have a much smaller sitting area. So, I didn't bother to sit on it anymore.

I also decided to take a look at the drainage ditches that I used to like playing in so much in the winter when it snowed, and I discovered that the drainage ditches had also shrunk and were a lot shallower than I remembered them being the first time we were in Rainy River.

I learned a few things from these experiences: Young children grow faster than honeysuckle bushes, tree stumps and drainage ditches shrink over time, and you need to understand that sometimes you lose your hiding places and favorite places to sit and play in the snow. The animals and birds probably feel the same way when their natural habitats are destroyed by people clearing land for farming or for building homes. Without a place to hide, I was going to have to face the reality of living in Rainy River as a big girl, and just deal with it.

Play Time

I used to play outside the house when school wasn't in session. And the kids in town used to play in each other's front yards. There was a house nearby that had a white picket fence around their yard. I was told that the owners of that house didn't want anybody walking on their grass, which I suppose is why they put up the fence in the first place. I learned a general rule early on in Rainy River that I was not to walk on anybody else's grass unless I was invited, whether or not there was a fence. We used to play mostly across the street in a nice yard which didn't have a fence, and the owner didn't mind if we did so.

The girls in Rainy River used to have a special way of counting the Robin birds in the spring, when they were migrating. They would count how many male Robins they saw, the ones with the bright red breasts. Whoever counted the most male Robins each spring became the "winner". Whenever they saw a Robin, they would push their thumb into the center of the palm of their left hand, and then make a fist with the right hand and smash down into the open palm of the left hand and add another one to the count.

I remember the little girls in Rainy River showing me buttercups, and ripping off one petal at a time and saying, "He loves me, he loves me not, he loves me, he loves me not".

Another game that the girls used to play was to take a ball into in a back alley behind one of the bake shops. They would take turns throwing and catching the ball in various ways. If you caught the ball you stayed in the game. If you didn't catch the ball you were out of the game. Each round, you did something harder and harder with the ball, to make sure that there would eventually be one winner.

Our Non Jewish Neighbors

We had very nice neighbors in Rainy River. I remember that one of my classmates at school was the daughter of the Pastor of the Protestant Church that was across the street from our house on the corner. The Pastor and his family lived in a large house near the Church. Their daughter had a birthday party once and I was invited to the party. I remember that they were sitting in the dining room, and I saw olives for the first time, and they had a red color inside. However, at that time I didn't know that they were olives, or even what olives were since I had never seen olives before.

I thought that they looked interesting and took a couple of them and put them on my plate. I smelled them, and I didn't like the way they smelled. I didn't know what to do with them, but I knew that I didn't want to eat them. So I took them in my hand, and when nobody was watching I "accidentally" dropped them on the floor one at a time while everyone else was busy talking.

I figured that nobody noticed, and nobody said anything to me about it. Thank goodness nobody noticed. I had successfully dodged another challenging situation, and lived to attend the next birthday party.

Next to that house lived the young lady who gave piano lessons. Near that house was a large house with a very large yard, and the kids in the town used to go there to play a game called "it", which I will explain a little later.

Near that house there was another big house where the husband of the house had been killed in an accident on the railroad. The widow was very sad about losing her husband. My mother used to hire one of their sons to do things for us on the Sabbath. In those days, we didn't have the luxury of having electric timers that could be used to turn the lights on and off on a Friday night or on Saturday during the day. And if nobody put wood into the stove, the fire would go out and we would be cold and not be able to heat up food on Friday night or Saturday.

My mother paid him ahead of time during the week to come turn off the lights on Friday night and feed the stove on Friday night and Saturday morning, since we were not allowed to pay anyone on the Sabbath itself to do work for us. Wherever we lived, my mother always found somebody who wasn't Jewish to help us out and do these things. Also, in Winnipeg, her father Rabbi Kahanovitch was always able to find girls from the neighborhood to come turn the lights on and off in the house. People were always willing to do this because they could use the money, but I think that they were also trying to be friendly and helpful.

When I first came to Rainy River, I was a very talkative child. My mother told me years later about something that I used to do which showed my desire to talk to people. Since I knew that my father was a dentist, I used to stand at the corner where the drug store was, and when anybody walked by I would tell them that there was a new dentist in town, and that he was my father. Evidently, this was my own original idea because nobody told me to do that. People in town saw what I was doing and told my mother about it. I don't think I ever mentioned it to my mother, so other people must have told her. Looking back on it, maybe it was a sign that I should go into sales and marketing as a career.

One time, I visited a girl in town who had an easel for writing. I had never seen one before and was very impressed. It had two sides to it. One side had a blackboard with the alphabet letters going around the blackboard. And the other side had paper hanging down so that you could write on it.

In that same house, I remember seeing a wood burning stove, but the pipe that carried the smoke from the stove was visible in the kitchen, not hidden inside the wall, and went up the ceiling into the next floor. In the house where we lived, you could see the stove, but you couldn't see any pipe for the smoke. So it must have been built into the wall. In that other house, the pipe was exposed, and it went straight up to the second floor.

In our house there were no radiators to provide heat. In the middle of the floor there was a metal grate, and it was very pretty. It had very pretty designs on it. It was made out of metal, but it wasn't simple looking. It was in the hallway that led to all of the bedrooms. But there was only one of them. So, that is why it was so cold in the winter.

There was a furnace in the basement of our house that generated the heat that came out of the grate in the hallway floor. The furnace burned wood, not coal. In the autumn or end of the summer, a wagon would come pulled by horses, and the wagon was filled with cut pieces of tree trunks. And they would leave a pile of tree branches up against the barn. In the summertime, the wagon with the horses would bring ice. There was a big room behind the kitchen, and the only thing in it was an ice box. It had a door so you could put just a few things in it. It was not very tall. A man would come and put a big hunk of ice in the top and covered it. As it stayed there it melted, and the water would go into a pan which would need to be emptied from time to time. I never saw anyone ever emptying the pan, but I knew that it must have been done on a regular basis.

In Rainy River, the ice that they brought in the summertime came from the river. They would cut it from the river and store it in a building somewhere. In the wintertime, I remember seeing someone sitting on a little chair on the ice in the middle of the river with a fishing pole. There were fish were swimming around underneath the ice, and you could catch fish in the winter.

There were back alleys in town that the ice and wood delivery people would use to lead their horses and wagons. They didn't travel on the main roads. One time in the summer, I was wandering around in a back alley behind one of the streets, and I saw that a barn had burned. At that time, people had horses. Generally, nobody had cars yet. So, a lot of houses had barns in the back to keep the horses. In the vicinity of the small, burned barn, there was a funny smell in the air. I asked someone why it smelled that way, and they explained that there was a horse in the barn when the fire happened. Horses get scared when there is a fire, and they refuse to come out of their barn. What I was smelling was the odor of cooked horse meat.

There was a big church across the street from where we lived, and the daughter of the Pastor was in school with me. One day her father brought out a sort of chair with two big wheels on it, and he attached it to the horse. It also had a bench that you could sit on. He picked me up and put me on the bench. From that vantage point, I could see the rear end of the horse. I just sat there for a little while, looking at the rear end of the horse, and then he took me off. I actually found that interesting. I suppose it gave me a different perspective of what a horse looks like while sitting behind it on a horse buggy. I remember that the horse was dark brown, and it grew a very thick, bushy tail in the summertime.

When I first went to school, the teacher would make all the

students stay quiet, and only talk when she pointed to them. Around that time, when I was seven years old or so, I remember one of my aunts telling me that old saying that little children should be seen and not heard. The teacher telling the kids to be quiet must have made a very strong impression on me, because I stopped talking much in class as well as outside of school. It took all of the spontaneity out of me, and most likely ruined my chances for a sales career.

One day, my grade four teacher in Rainy River told the class that the Jews killed Jesus. After school I went home and told my mother about what the teacher had said. By this point, I had been back to Winnipeg for some of the Jewish holidays, and I knew by then that there were other Jews in the world, and that we weren't the only ones on the planet.

My mother was very upset about what the teacher told the students in my class, and she went to talk with the teacher and ask her why she said that to the class. The teacher told my mother that that is what her Priest had told her.

My mother decided to write to one of her relatives who was a Rabbi, and ask him whether he had any books about what actually happened around the time of Jesus and the circumstances surrounding his death, and asked whether he could send her one or more of those books.

My mother told the teacher that the Romans killed Jesus. But she wanted to have something in print that supported that account of history to show to the teacher. I don't remember whether my mother received any books about it, but she went and spoke with the teacher anyway.

Soon after this interaction of my mother with my teacher, I noticed that I was no longer being invited to birthday parties. I thought that perhaps the other girls were just getting older and didn't have birthday parties anymore, but later I realized that it was probably because of what the teacher told the other students, and because my mother had complained about it.

Bedtime

There was a period of time when I was a little girl when I thought that my parents didn't like me. I started thinking what I could do to make them like me. I couldn't think of anything to accomplish that goal, but I reasoned that if my parents thought that I had died for some reason, then my parents would at least feel sorry that they weren't nice to me when I was still alive. I remember that my mother would come up and check on me before I went to sleep in the evenings. I came up with the idea of trying to lie very still under the covers, and holding my breath as a way of pretending that I was dead, and not to actually be dead. But I couldn't hold my breath for very long, so that strategy didn't work.

I remember hearing my parents having heated discussions sometimes after I went upstairs to my bedroom. They might have been discussing the war in Europe, or perhaps the fact that some of my father's patients weren't paying their bills. Years later, I found out that there was about 2,000 dollars owing to my father for dental work he had done. Compared to 25 dollars per month for rent, that was a lot of money.

Many of the people who lived in Rainy River at that time were very poor and didn't have enough money to pay for dental work. Instead of paying cash they would bring my father fish that they had caught. Maybe that's why we had so many fish swimming in the bathtub, and my mother didn't have to buy fish to make her gefilte fish.

Making My Bed

My mother told me to make my bed in the morning, and straighten out the sheets and blanket. There was something that fitted on top of the blankets, and I was told that I needed to straighten that out also. The bed was a double size bed, and it was situated in the corner of the bedroom, so there were only two sides of the bed that you could reach without pulling it away from the walls.

Still being a relatively short child then, I had to crawl all over the bed to straighten out the sheets. I was very proud that I had done this, since it was a lot of work for me, and I put my best effort into the task. It was quite exhausting, and I was looking forward to my mother showering praises on me for my fantastic ability to make my bed so nicely. Then my mother came in to take a look and inspect how well I had made the bed.

There were some creases in the material on the top of the bed because I had been crawling all over it to stretch the material over the entire bed, and I couldn't stand next to the two sides of the bed that were against the walls in the corner of the room. My mother noticed the creases and pulled on the cover that went on top of the blanket to get rid of the creases. And I didn't receive the shower of praises that I was hoping for.

For some reason that experience stuck in my mind all of these years. I remember being very upset by it, and I told myself that I would never make my bed again. If it wasn't good enough for my mother, then why bother? After that, I never made my bed again in Rainy River.

The Spooky Staircase

My bedroom had a door in it that wasn't a closet door. When I opened it, I could see that there were stairs that led upwards, probably to the attic of the house. The steps in the staircase were very narrow and high. It looked like a very strange and scary staircase, unlike any other staircase that I had ever seen.

I was afraid of those stairs, and didn't want to go up and see where they led, so I never tried going up them. One night, after I had fallen asleep, I had a dream that I heard footsteps of someone coming down those stairs from the attic. The door slowly opened, and an old lady peered out from behind the door. I was scared, because the old lady must have been up in the attic all this time, and nobody knew about her. I woke up, and then I realized that it was just a dream.

After having this dream, I was afraid to go to bed and fall asleep. I didn't want to hear those footsteps, and I didn't want to see anyone looking at me from behind that door. Most evenings, while my parents were still in the kitchen talking about what happened during the day, they would send me upstairs to go to bed. But I was afraid to go to bed for a long time because of the dream, and I would just lie in bed with my eyes open hoping not to hear the footsteps and see the old lady in the staircase.

A Scary Halloween

Near the beginning of our stay in Rainy River, the time came for people to celebrate Halloween. I didn't know anything about it, and I had no idea what Halloween involved. The day after Halloween, I saw that people had written something on the outside wall of a store that was across the street from the drug store. There were no windows on that side of the store. It had been a nice clean wall before, but that day it was covered with writing, and I remember thinking that it was terrible that people would do that to someone's store. I only found out later that this was normal, and it happened every year.

One Halloween, a few years later when we were still living in Rainy River, I found out that the children in town went around to people's houses and got dressed up in costumes and got candy, so I thought it would be fun to join them and do that also. My parents let me venture out that year on Halloween night. It was a dark night, a very dark night. No moon was visible in the sky. The darkness added a certain, very appropriate, spookiness to the night.

All of a sudden, I saw something strange moving in the sky. I had no idea what it was. I had never seen anything like it before. It turned out to be the Northern Lights. It filled up the whole sky, with lots of colors which kept moving. I got really scared by it. I felt like the earth was moving underneath me, and I didn't like that feeling. I went back home and never went out again on Halloween because of that experience.

Maybe I had overreacted, but after I went back to Winnipeg once our stay in Rainy River was over, I realized that Jewish children normally don't participate in Trick or Treat activities. Not because of the scary Northern Lights, but because of the non-Jewish religious significance of Halloween.

The Circus

A circus came to Rainy River once. The whole town came out to see the circus, and it was very crowded. The circus was a lot simpler in those days compared to the circuses of today. I remember going there with my mother, and I remember seeing a merry-go-round and the music in the merry-go-round was very loud. The owner of the circus was a Jewish man, and he became friendly with my parents because of the fact that we were also Jewish.

When he saw that I kept looking at the merry-go-round, the owner offered to let me to ride on the merry-go-round for free. The problem was that the horses on the merry-go-round moved up and down, and I was scared to sit on one of the moving horses. I was afraid that I would fall off the horse and get hurt. So, the owner picked me up and put me on a bench which didn't go up and down.

My mother invited him to come over and visit with us in our house, and to share a meal that my mother had prepared. The owner of the circus gave me a tiny necklace with tiny beads made from amber stone which had a brown color. I don't know for sure, but my guess is that the necklace probably came from somewhere in Russia.

Back in School

Having spent a year in Winnipeg attending grade three, I went back to school in Rainy River as a grade four student. The building that housed the grade three and above students was a large brick or stone building, compared to the small wooden house that housed the grade one and two students. However, as it was in the small house, the room that I was in for grade four had two grades sitting in it: grades three and four.

The students who were in the grade four half of the room had already spent their previous year in grade three on the other side of the room, and the same teacher taught both sides of the room. So the students whom I sat with in grade four had already spent a year learning from that teacher. In that sense, I was a newbie in the room, and it felt a little strange being the only new student in grade four.

The teacher had a unique system for teaching arithmetic that I had never seen before. She would make a jumble of numbers in a circle on the chalk board. Then, she would stand holding a long pointy stick, and she would point to one number and say "plus", and then touch another number and you had to yell out the answer. And then she would say "times" and touch a different number. You had to calculate the answer in your head, and then shout it out. Looking back on it, this was a good way to force you to think about numbers and basic arithmetic in your head, rather than writing the numbers down on a piece of paper and thinking about the calculations that way.

The grade three students were taught using the same method as the grade four students. But I couldn't keep up with the other students in grade four because they didn't teach arithmetic that way in Winnipeg, and I just couldn't do it fast enough. I felt very stupid because I couldn't calculate the answers fast enough. Luckily for me, that teacher was the only one that I ever encountered who taught arithmetic using that unusual system, and I never needed to do fast arithmetic calculations in my head like that again.

Interestingly, that teacher was also very strict about cleanliness. In our notebooks we had to write a list of things that we needed to do in the morning, like washing our hands, washing our face, and even washing behind our ears. Nobody had ever told me to wash behind my ears, so that was kind of a shocker. I wondered whether I was the only child who had never heard about washing behind their ears.

One thing that I liked about the classroom was that if you were given something to do, and you finished it quickly, you could go to the back of the room and pick a book and take it back to your desk and read the book at your desk until the other students finished the assignment. There was no library in Rainy River, so this was a nice way to get to read some books. In fact, the school in Rainy River was the only place that I saw children's books while I was there.

Another thing that the grade four teacher did was to bring pussy willow branches that she had cut from a bush where they were growing into the classroom in the springtime, and she would put them in a tall jar. The buds on the branches were closed initially. But over a period of days and weeks, they would open up and make the fuzzy little things that pussy willows are known for. The long, tall branches were situated on a small table, and they really made an oversized impression in the classroom. It took some time for the hard husks to open and reveal the soft while pussy willows inside, but once they did open they were very beautiful to look at.

One time she brought a little bowl of water into the classroom in the early spring, with very tiny fish eggs in it. Over a period of weeks, they turned into tiny fish – guppies perhaps. These two things, the pussy willow twigs and the fish eggs, were very interesting to watch as they developed, and they showed us how nature was changing as springtime progressed.

More Scary Sights and Sounds

One day I was walking to school in the morning. I had gotten a late start that morning for some reason. The town was deserted, and very quiet, because by then all of the other children had gone to school and were in their classes, and all of the adults who had jobs were already at work. It was snowing lightly, and the ground was completely white because of the covering of fresh snow. There were no trees or bushes, just a large flat area covered with snow. This was the area that I had to walk through in order to get to the school. There were no footprints in the snow because everyone had already gone wherever they were going to go earlier that morning. The sky was also white because of the snow. It was just white everywhere, and in a way it was very peaceful and serene.

There was so much snow that I couldn't see where the special wooden boards were that acted like little bridges near the street intersections, so that people could easily walk over the drainage ditches at the sides of the streets without falling in. Not being able to see where those boards were made me extra scared, because I could fall into the drainage ditch at any moment, like an animal falling into a trap.

Then, all of a sudden, I heard a faint sound, a strange sound. And it gradually got louder and louder. I wasn't sure what was making the sound, and I wasn't even sure where it was coming from. But I knew that I hadn't heard this kind of sound before. It sounded like a kind of shrieky noise. Maybe it was an injured animal? Maybe it was a bird in distress?

Finally, I noticed something off in the distance. It was gradually getting closer, and as it got closer it looked bigger and bigger. Then I realized that there was something that looked like smoke coming out of it. Perhaps it was some kind of fire breathing monster? I was scared. I kept watching it as it got closer, and the sound kept getting louder.

When it was not too far away, I realized that it was a train. The sound that I was hearing was the train's whistle, which made a sort of shrieking noise. The train engine was shooting steam into the air, and it looked like a big plume of smoke. But, of course, steam engines give off steam, not smoke. It was the first time that I had seen a train moving along the tracks. Since the ground was covered with snow, all I could see was the train, and it looked very spooky, as though it was gliding through the snow. After that experience, I got used to seeing the trains, and they didn't seem so spooky anymore.

A Prickly Situation

We used to play a game called "it". There was a tree in the yard across the street. One child would be selected as the "it" person. That person would stand facing the tree with their eyes closed and count to 10. While that child was counting to 10, the other children would run and hide nearby. Then, the "it" child would open their eyes and try to find the other children. Each of the other children would try to run back to the tree and touch it and yell "home free". If you were able to do that, then you were safe from becoming the "it". If you couldn't find anyone before they all got back to the tree, then you were the "loser". Then the game would go on with the "loser" being "it" again.

The farther the "it" child moved away from the tree in order to try to find the other children, the higher the chance that the children who were hiding could run toward the tree and touch it and yell "home free". If the "it" child found one of the other children before all of the other children had made it back to the tree, then that other child would become the new "it", and the process would keep repeating until they all got tired of playing.

I wasn't very good at this game, and I couldn't find people who were hiding very often. Since I almost never caught anybody, I ended up being "it" many times. I suppose the positive side of that was that I got a lot of exercise running around trying to find the other children.

One day it was my turn to be "it". I stood facing the tree, and I closed my eyes and held onto the tree, and I counted to 10. Then I opened my eyes and tried to find the other children. I started looking around, but I couldn't see anybody at all. I looked around very carefully at all of the places where the other children had hidden themselves in the past. This time, it seemed that everyone had hidden themselves very well, much better than any time in the past. Then I saw a strange looking animal I had never seen before. I looked at the animal, and it looked back at me. Long, thin bristles started rising on the animal. It was a very strange little animal, and it looked like a ball of bristles.

I was very scared and thought that the animal would run at me and attack me. The animal was in between me and our house across the street. I froze. I didn't know what to do. Apparently, everyone else had disappeared, perhaps as a kind of joke, and I realized that I was all alone. And I was all alone facing a deadly prickly monster! It turned itself into a round ball with lots of prickly looking things sticking out of it.

Later I was told that the scary looking animal was called a porcupine, but at that time I didn't know what it was. I had never seen a porcupine before, and nobody had ever spoken about them. Maybe porcupines were rather rare in town.

I don't remember what happened to the porcupine, or how I got out of the situation. My mind just draws a blank when I try to recollect the details of what happened next. But I must have survived because I am still alive, writing this book many years later. I never saw that porcupine again. Perhaps it was just as scared of me as I was of it. And perhaps the reason that the other children disappeared was that they had seen the porcupine and ran away scared without bothering to tell me.

The Town Fair

In the summer, Rainy River used to hold a town fair. I remember attending the fair and seeing children who had bicycles and tricycles that were decorated with crepe paper. The children took crepe paper of many different colors, and attached pieces of them to the spokes of their bicycle wheels. It must have been a special kind of decoration that was done specially for the town fair because I never saw that type of decoration at any other time of the year.

I did notice, however, that some people used to use this kind of crepe paper at Christmas time to make circles, and then connect those circles into a long chain, and would use the chains of crepe paper to decorate the insides of their homes. One time, a little girl on our street invited me into her house in the winter, and I remember seeing a Christmas tree with those kinds of decorations hanging on the tree.

Getting back to the town fair, everybody came out to a big open space in town. There were lots of tables, and the women brought large amounts of food in glass jars called Mason jars. There were judges who would taste the food and announce the winners of the best tasting foods. It didn't cost anything to attend the town fair, and I don't remember there being any animals at the fair. Only people. And lots of food.

Books

In our house there were some Hebrew books because my father was teaching me to read Hebrew, and we needed to have some Hebrew books for doing that. But in general, we had very few books in our house. My mother took out a subscription to the local monthly book club, so that we had some books, but they were all in English. One of the books that we had was a very big, thick and heavy dictionary, which was a premium prize that we received for starting a subscription.

I remember reading somewhere while I was in Rainy River that American movie actresses had to walk very straight and tall. And one of the exercises that they had to do was to walk with a book on their head and balance it so that it wouldn't fall off. It sounded like a good exercise, so I decided that I would try to walk with that big dictionary on my head so that I could learn to walk straight. But it was so heavy that I was afraid that the book might fall down and get damaged, so I decided not to do it. I didn't consider that if that book fell on my foot it might have injured my toes, and it's probably a good thing that I didn't try balancing the big dictionary on my head because of that possibility.

My mother used to read me a book by Leo Rosten with stories about a fictional character named Hyman Kaplan. It was written as though someone was speaking English with a Yiddish accent. My mother would read it to me on the sofa, and it sounded so funny because nobody else in Rainy River spoke like that.

Animals

At one point while we were living in Rainy River, my parents were given a little puppy from someone in town as a present. But we had to give it back to the owners of the mother dog because it was too young to be on its own. I remember seeing it trying to eat the grass in our yard outside our house. I don't think dogs are supposed to eat the grass. I guess we didn't really know how to take care of puppies.

There were a lot of horses in town. People used the horses to pull things, like ice trucks. Back in those days, people didn't have electric refrigerators and freezers, and the only way that they could keep their food fresh during the warmer months was to buy blocks of ice and put them in a special ice box that would keep the food cold. It's probably a good thing that my parents didn't get a pet horse. If we couldn't take care of a tiny puppy, we certainly were not going to be able to take care of a big horse. It would probably have eaten all of the grass in our yard before we realized what was happening.

Day Trips

Every now and then we took day trips outside of Rainy River to explore different areas. I remember once we took a trip out to the countryside. A man with a car that looked like a Model T, with square sides and top, drove us. When we got to our destination, there was a little river, a very shallow little river. It was a bright sunny day, and you could see all of the different colored stones under the water in the river. What an amazing and beautiful sight!

On another trip, someone took us to a farm where they were raising minks, and the minks were in cages. At one point I reached out to pet them, but someone quickly pulled my hand back, because the mink would have probably bitten my little fingers.

On another trip, we went to visit a country store run by my father's brother. I remember it being very cold, during the wintertime. His daughter had red hair. My paternal grandfather Helman had a red moustache. My father's hair, whatever was left of it, and his mustache, also had a little red in it. It must have been a Helman tradition to have reddish hair.

One time, when we were in the country visiting my uncle's store, I had to go to the bathroom. They didn't have indoor plumbing, and it was bitter cold outside. Too cold for me to go outside and use the outhouse that was in the back yard. Instead, they brought out a little round white pot with a handle on it. People used to keep it under the bed, so that in the middle of the night they could take care of business. Everyone was sitting in the kitchen at that moment. Someone brought out the pot with the handle, and put it under the table for me to use, but it was very cold. It was white enameled metal, so it was very, very cold. While I was sitting on the pot, literally, under the kitchen table, I could see people's legs.

The House With The Glass Door

I liked to wander around town to explore Rainy River and see what the other houses looked like. On Main Street near the river, there was a house with a very interesting front door. There was a large oval piece of glass that was inserted into the central part of the door. It was clear glass, so you could look right into the inside of the house. It was a special type of glass, with mitered edges. But other than that, it provided very little privacy. You could see it clearly from the street.

All other houses that I saw had solid wood doors. I remember being so interested by the glass door that I boldly walked up to the house and knocked on the front door. A nice lady opened up the front door and I told her that she had a very lovely front door. Unfortunately, my positive compliment wasn't enough to qualify me to be invited inside the house, so that was the end of that.

Shabbat in Rainy River

Shabbat is the Hebrew word that means the Sabbath in English. The word means "rest" or "cessation of work". Shabbat starts every Friday evening a little before sunset, and my mother would light two special white candles in the dining room in honor of Shabbat. One of the things that a Jewish wife does in a traditional religious Jewish home is to light a pair of candles on Friday afternoon, 18 minutes before sunset, and my mother tried very hard to maintain that tradition, even though we were in a town that had no Jewish community to speak of, other than ourselves.

My parents also observed the Jewish Kosher food laws very carefully, but it was always a challenge to find food that we could eat without violating those laws. There weren't any Kosher meat stores or grocery stores in Rainy River. My maternal grandmother, Rabbi Israel Kahanovitch's wife, used to go downtown in Winnipeg to buy Kosher beef and send it via the train in a package to Rainy River. Unfortunately, there was no refrigeration on the train, so in the warmer weather the meat would go bad by the time we received it. But my mother didn't tell me at the time that the meat was going bad. I only found out many years later. I guess she didn't want me to be upset about it at the time.

My grandmother also used to send Kosher chickens to us in Rainy River, so that we could have chicken for the Shabbat meal on Friday evening. A Kosher chicken is a chicken that has been slaughtered in the traditional way that is virtually painless to the chicken. It is a custom among many Jews to eat some form of cooked chicken on Friday night for dinner, and we were able to maintain that custom thanks to my resourceful grandmother.

There were many times when we had some small leftover pieces of cooked chicken from the Friday night dinners, and my mother had a wonderful recipe for using those leftovers. She would chop up the cooked chicken pieces and mix then with some fried onion. Then she would take some mashed potatoes and use the chicken and onion mixture as a filling inside potato pancakes which she formed from the mashed potatoes. And then she would fry them on top of the stove. They were delicious. She only used to do this on Sundays because there wasn't much chicken meat left over after the Shabbat meals, and by the end of the day on Sunday the pancakes were all eaten.

My mother never made this recipe again after we left Rainy River and went back to Winnipeg. I suppose that we didn't have enough leftovers from Friday night dinners in Winnipeg, so there weren't any leftover chicken bits to turn into something yummy. But those potato pancakes stuffed with chicken and fried onion tasted so good that I won't ever forget them.

For the holiday of Passover, in the springtime, we would travel back to Winnipeg and have Seders at Rabbi Kahanovitch's house while his wife was still alive. Unfortunately, as I mentioned previously, she died in 1940. I remember seeing a little, tiny lady at the Seders, and that must have been her. She was under five feet tall. Rabbi Kahanovitch was not much taller. She had 12 children, but only eight of them survived. The survival rate of newborn babies was much lower in those days compared to today.

Kosher Food

When I was living in Rainy River, I knew something about what Kosher food was, although I didn't know all of the rules yet at that point. There are many rules that you have to learn about, and follow, if you want to fully observe the Kosher food laws. One of the consequences of us eating only Kosher food was that I was only allowed to eat the cake at birthday parties and nothing else. During our last year in Rainy River, another Jewish family came to Rainy River. At last, we weren't the only Jewish family in Rainy River! It was very exciting. I remember being invited to their house and they made Vorscht sandwiches. Vorscht is the Yiddish word for processed meats, like salami. That was the first time I had seen salami.

Until that other family moved to Rainy River, not only was my family the only Jewish family in the town, but I also thought that my family was the only Jewish family in the whole world.

In general, I couldn't eat food in other kids' houses when they invited me to birthday parties. I didn't realize what was going on behind the scenes. Apparently, before the party took place, my mother would speak with the mother of the birthday girl about Kosher food and explain what I could and could not eat, so there was no problem. The other parents were very understanding, and prepared food that I could eat, so I wouldn't be left out of the celebration.

In the River

Someone once told me that there was a man who taught kids how to swim in the river. He would carry them above the water while wading into the river, and then would drop them into the river and tell them to try to swim. I'm not sure that is the best way to teach a child how to swim, and I never saw that myself, but I didn't want to have any part of that. What if I were dropped in the river and couldn't figure out how to swim? I didn't like to think about that possibility.

I once saw some kids during the summer at the river with what looked like homemade fishing poles. Some kids stripped the bark off a branch, and left the green inside of the branch exposed. Then, they gave it to me and told me that I could use it as a fishing pole. I tried using it to catch fish, but I didn't catch anything. I don't remember seeing any of the other children actually catch any fish either. Probably most of the kids were just pretending to fish.

Visiting Friends

One time, one of the girls from school took me to visit her house. Behind the main house was another house that she said was a dairy, where her father managed the milk deliveries to the town. It smelled terrible in there, a very sour smell. I remember running out of that building very quickly. I suppose if you work with milk every day, you eventually get used to it.

Another time, I visited one of my school friends who lived in a house with no basement, which was probably built that way to avoid having to deal with the possibility of a wet basement. The yard was lower than the sidewalk, so rain water tended to collect there. Perhaps it was one of the first houses built in Rainy River. When it snowed, that yard was one of the last places where there was still snow after the snow had melted almost everywhere else.

Another kid invited me to their house in the middle of the winter. The back yard had flooded, and the water was all frozen. A group of kids tried "skating" on the ice using just their shoes because none of the children had ice skates. I tried imitating what they were doing, but I just kept falling down, and I didn't like that. My career as an ice skater ended right there and then.

Eating Meals

When I was in Rainy River, breakfast was usually porridge, also known as oatmeal. My mother used to get up very early in the morning to cook the porridge so that it would be soft enough to eat. It took a long time to cook, and they didn't have instant oatmeal in those days.

Once, when I was eating some cooked fresh fish, a bone got stuck in my mouth and I didn't know what to do. I think that my father either told me to eat some bread, or he reached into my mouth and pulled out the bone. After that experience, I was very, very careful when eating cooked fish, and I made sure to cut it up into very small pieces so that I wouldn't accidentally each any fish bones.

In addition to making her own gefilte fish, my mother also used to make her own cottage cheese in Rainy River. I'm not sure how she did it. Milk was delivered to the back of the house in glass bottles. When it was very cold the milk came separated, not homogenized. It would separate into cream on the top and milk on the bottom. The delivery van didn't have heat in it, so in the winter the cream would rise up above the top of the bottle. There was a little piece of paper over the bottle opening, but very often it would get pushed up by the expanding milk and cream.

The Hotel

There was a hotel in Rainy River, near the railway station. I remember being in it once. One of my friends from school was the daughter of the couple who ran the hotel. She brought me into the hotel, and she showed me a room on the second floor. The door was open, but I didn't go in the room, and didn't see anybody. But I could see the curtains on the window. They had a lot of nice big flowers, different colors, with a light background. The light from outside the window gave you a lot of light in the room. It looked very pretty. But the floors in the hotel were very creaky sounding. They must have been old wooden floors.

The Foundation

When I was in Rainy River, and not in school, I used to like wandering around the town and exploring the area. Once I came across what looked like an old foundation of a very small building, basically some bricks or stones, arranged in a square. This was a little bit outside of the main town area. I used to read that the Romans had set up camps for their soldiers in many of the places that they were, so my mind started imagining that perhaps this was part of an old Roman camp. Looking back on it, it probably wasn't the foundation of a Roman building. But I had heard about the Romans and how they spread their empire over a large part of the world. And Roman artifacts have been found in various parts of Canada. So, who knows? Maybe the Romans visited Canada when they were looking for a new place to take a vacation.

Part Five

Back to Winnipeg

In a New Practice

After living in Rainy River for several years, my father had finally gotten enough experience as a dentist by 1941 that he was able to find employment as a dentist back in Winnipeg.

When we left Rainy River to head back to Winnipeg, it happened suddenly. I don't remember there being much discussion about it. Poof! In almost no time at all, we were back in Winnipeg. I had been in grade four in Rainy River, and the school year wasn't quite over. My parents didn't even wait for the summer to come, deciding to go back to Winnipeg in the springtime. So I entered grade four in Winnipeg toward end of the school year.

I remember that I had a teacher in Winnipeg with a terrible temper. She would walk up and down between the aisles of desks, scrutinizing all of the student notebooks and their handwriting. The children in school at that time were writing with pen and ink. The pens had metal nibs on the end. Every desk had a little glass container that fitted into the desk. One of the school kids would come every day and fill each glass container with ink. You had to dip your pen into the ink, and then you could write with the pen.

If that teacher saw a blotch, meaning too much ink was used on the pen, the teacher would take the whole notepad and throw it across the room. I guess there wasn't time to remove the offending piece of paper and just throw it across the room. Needless to say, those days that I had to spend at the end of grade four in Winnipeg were not the greatest. But at least the days passed quickly, and I only had to deal with that teacher for a short period of time.

It actually made sense for us to move back to Winnipeg, even though it interrupted my schooling, so that we could be part of a Jewish community with synagogues, Jewish schools, and easily available Kosher food. Living in Rainy River was interesting and definitely a learning experience, but being observant Jews, we were a little like a group of fish out of water.

Unfortunately, starting a new dental practice required a large investment of money, which my parents didn't have. So, instead, my father worked as a dentist within the office of another successful dentist in town. And he remained at that dental practice for the rest of his career as a dentist.

One of the nice things that my father enjoyed about working as a dentist in Rainy River, even though he didn't make much money doing so, was that he worked for himself. That gave him a lot of flexibility in terms of setting his working hours, and how he managed his dental practice. In general, working for someone else comes with lots of rules that limit what you can do, as well as less flexibility in terms of being able to spend time with one's family. So, in that sense, having his own dental practice in Rainy River allowed my father to spend more time with my mother and me, for which I am very grateful.

Strange To Relate

Some interesting things used to happen when my father worked as a dentist in Winnipeg. I remember that the farmers from the villages surrounding Winnipeg were so busy during the growing season, which was mainly in the spring, summer and fall, that they didn't have time to go into town for treatment of their teeth.

Every winter, the farmers would come into the city. Many of them saw my father for treatment, which they weren't able to do at other times of the year. The farmers were very tough men, and many of them would ask my father to just pull out all of their teeth and replace them with dentures so that they wouldn't keep having problems with their teeth.

Another interesting thing used to happen almost every winter around New Year. Inevitably, some men would get so drunk from celebrating the New Year holiday that they would throw up in the toilet, and not realize that their dentures were being ejected from their mouths in the process. After accidentally flushing their dentures down the toilet, they would place frantic phone calls to my father asking him to make emergency replacements for them.

The Army Dentist

I want to say a little more about my father, as a tribute to his memory and his generosity as a human being. I remember that when he was going to dental college in Toronto, he taught Bar Mitzvah boys to read Hebrew as a way to make some money.

Someone told me that my father used to say that if you have a toothache when you eat or drink cold foods, then it means that the condition of your tooth isn't so bad. But if you have a toothache when you eat or drink hot foods, then it could mean that the tooth is infected, because the heat can cause the infected area to expand and that puts pressure on the nerve in the tooth. It sounds like an interesting theory, but I don't know whether or not it's true.

When I was a little girl, World War Two was just beginning. I really don't remember hearing anything about what was going on in Europe at the time. It took a while for news from Europe to trickle into Canada. Other than the incident where some of the boys called another boy "Hitler" at the school in Rainy River just because the boy had the first name "Adolph", I wasn't really aware of how bad the situation was becoming in Europe.

Soon after we had moved back to Winnipeg, the extent of the devastation of World War Two, and the destruction of many Jewish communities and lives in Europe, were becoming increasingly clear to people living in Canada. Instead of living a comfortable life working as a dentist in Canada, while his fellow Jews were being killed in Europe, my father wanted to join the Canadian army as a dentist to help out in the way that he knew best. He also wanted to do this to help pay back Canada for being so nice to him and his family, and letting them come into Canada.

Living in Canada, we could listen to the BBC news that was broadcast from England. Whatever information was allowed to be broadcast in England about the war was also sent to Canada. My father lived through World War One in Zelva, so he knew what war meant and how destructive it could be. And he had lived through a number of Pogroms that were specifically targeted against the Jews who lived in that area.

The experiences that my father had in Europe made him decide to apply for admittance to the Dental Corps of the Canadian Army. I remember hearing that phrase, the "Dental Corps", at an early age and thinking that it sounded funny. But in reality, it was a very serious venture that he was volunteering for.

At that point in my father's life, he was too old to be drafted. So, he had to volunteer to go overseas. In fact, as I recall, all Canadian forces who went overseas volunteered to go overseas. Nobody was forced to go.

When my father went to the Army recruitment office to volunteer for service overseas, they gave him a medical examination. He was told that he had a hernia and needed to have it fixed, or he could not join the army. He immediately underwent the necessary surgery, which fixed the hernia, he healed up quickly, and he was ready to enlist. My father ended up serving in the Canadian army from 1942 to 1945.

He was one of the dentist soldiers who landed on the beach at Normandy one day after the first wave of soldiers who landed on D Day. The dentists were there to help the injured soldiers who had either lost teeth, or had parts of their jaws blown off from gunfire and explosions the day before.

The dentists were transported to the general area in ships. There were small boats that would come up next to the ship to take the dentists to the shore. My father was supposed to climb down the side of the ship that he was on using a rope ladder, and then jump off the bottom of the rope ladder, which was dangling just a few feet above the bottom of the small boat that was ready to take them ashore. He told me many years later that about halfway down the rope ladder he slipped and lost his footing, and he fell into the boat from a fairly high level. Miraculously, he survived the fall into the boat and wasn't seriously hurt, and luckily he didn't hurt anyone else or cause the small boat to sink.

Part of his training in the army was to learn how to drive a truck. There were a lot of gears in the truck, and he had to learn how to shift between all of those gears. They also did a lot of marching around, which was part of the training. Another thing he had to learn was how to use a compass to navigate his way around. As part of their training, the army would drive a bunch of the soldiers somewhere away from the camp at nighttime, and then tell them to find their way back to the camp using their compasses.

After serving in the Canadian Army, my father became a member of the General Monash Branch, #115, of the Royal Canadian Legion. According to the website of the Royal Canadian Legion, they are Canada's largest Veteran support and community service organization. Branch #115 was named after General Sir John Monash, who was a very successful Australian Jewish army commander during World War One.

After my father came back to Canada from the war in Europe, my parents discussed whether to set up a dental practice in one of the new suburbs around Winnipeg. However, it would take a long time before you could make any money if you set up your own dental office. My mother also suggested to my father that they should consider moving to Ottawa to set up an office. But my father didn't want to go to Ottawa, probably because there was a much larger Jewish community in Winnipeg.

I remember going with my mother to the train station to meet my father when he returned from the war in Europe. He came up to us and said, "Where's Toby?" He didn't recognize me! I had grown up and was a big girl by then. He had been in Europe for about three and a half years, and I must have looked very different than I did when he packed up and went to Europe in 1942.

In 1945, when my father returned, I was 12 years old. In those days, there were no Bat Mitzvahs in Winnipeg, so I didn't have one. Nowadays it is very common for Jewish girls to have a Bat Mitzvah ceremony at age 12. We were told in the Hebrew School that girls could start fasting on Yom Kippur and Tisha B'Av at the age of 12. Boys could start fasting at age 13. I remember that when I turned 12 years old I was very happy because I was finally able to fast on those special days. Once I reached that age, I didn't get hungry when I fasted, and it made those days much more meaningful.

After my father got back from Europe, he decided to stay in Winnipeg and work there. He belonged to a Jewish Dental Association in the Army. He could have asked them about a possible job, but that might have required a lot of travel or other things that would mean that he wouldn't be able to spend a lot of time with his family. My father was very much a family man, and he tried very hard to make time to spend with my mother and me.

Instead, my father got a job working for a local dentist who had an established dental practice, and he worked in that dentist's office. There were multiple dentists working there. He made around $25 per month plus 10% of whatever was charged. In those days, a filling cost a patient one dollar, so he made 10 cents for each cavity that he filled. The big money, apparently, was with false teeth, but my father wasn't assigned any of those.

The dental office moved at some point to the block where the department stores were located. There was a great big waiting room, and a big circular desk with women answering the phone. There was a laboratory where they made the false teeth. As I recall, it was a very big operation.

The dental patients liked my father very much. He worked very quickly, either because of his experience working as an army dentist, where you don't get much time to work on each injured soldier, or perhaps because he was paid so little from doing fillings. The faster he could do a filling, the more he could do in a day, and the more he would get paid. He would get phone calls in the middle of the night from his patients for emergency work that they needed done. Apparently his patients really liked him and the work that he did.

Many years later, when my late husband served as a congregational Rabbi at the Shaare Zedek synagogue on the West Side of Manhattan, New York City, my father once attended the Shabbat services in the synagogue on a Saturday morning, and he was given the honor of reading the Haftarah portion for that day. He had a beautiful voice, and he read it with much feeling. All the words were clear, and it was very musical. He read it in such a way that he seemed to be explaining what he was reading. He kept up with his Hebrew. He subscribed to the Hadoar magazine, in Winnipeg, to keep his Hebrew in good shape.

A Big Girl in a Big World

The experience of moving from Winnipeg to Rainy River and back, twice, helped me to realize the strength that I had inside of me, both as a person and as a Jew. I realized that I could get through almost anything and come out alive on the other end. I survived the strange noises that turned out to be a train, I survived the spooky Northern Lights, I survived the scary old woman who kept appearing in my dreams from behind the door to the attic, I survived being left alone by my playmates and facing a scary porcupine, I survived being left alone in the snowy ditch, I survived not being invited to the other girls' birthday parties, and I survived waiting for the train at 2:30 AM on a deserted train platform.

I also learned that I was, and still am, able to remain true to my Jewish roots in spite of living in a non-Jewish world. On the other hand, the experience also showed me that although I am Jewish, I am part of a larger world that includes many people who are not

Jewish. And it showed me that it is important to be aware of the fact that the world is a big place with many people from vastly different backgrounds and with different beliefs.

Rainy River taught me that there are people who are friendly no matter what their background or religion; and if they are willing to learn even a little bit about Jews and Judaism, then they come to appreciate the fact that Jews are people just like them, and are also part of the larger world around them. Rainy River taught me that we all need to tolerate each other, and try to understand each other's backgrounds and history. The world would be a better place if people put more emphasis on learning about others, and trying to live together in harmony, rather than living in division and discord.

I Will Return to You, Rainy River

I look back at my years in Rainy River as a very nice and pleasant time. There were big trees and a lot of shade in summertime, and it was very quiet. In Winnipeg, by contrast, there were almost no trees on the main streets and the bright sun was very hard to take. In comparison, Rainy River was like a little Paradise.

The last time I was in Rainy River, I was a little girl. A little girl who had grown quite a bit from being an even smaller girl. But I was still a little girl. It's been a long time since then. I recently celebrated my 90th birthday. I can't become a little girl again physically, and I can't actually travel to Rainy River anymore. But I can visit Rainy River in my mind.

When I was a child, I didn't have trouble falling asleep. And before I would go to bed, my mother would pull the sheets over my head and tell me softly to go to a place she used to call Lushke Park. Apparently that was an imaginary place where you could go in your dreams, and play and have fun.

Now that I am older, I sometimes do have trouble falling asleep. When that happens, I take a mental trip to Rainy River. It becomes my "Lushke Park". I can visualize in my mind walking around the streets, and I can name all the plants and the street names around the house where we used to live. I can see the horses pulling the ice wagon as they slowly walk down the back alleys. I can see the bakery and smell the fresh bread, and I can see the shoemaker shop and my father's dental office. I walk over to the school, and then back home again. Sometimes I am asleep before I get back to the house.

Near the end of the walk from the small school, the little girls show me buttercups and rip off one petal at a time and say, "He loves me, he loves me not, he loves me, he loves me not". I'm usually asleep before I get to that point. And then I arrive back home in our house in Rainy River and fall deeply asleep. This is how I am able to return to Rainy River whenever I want without travelling there by plane, by train or even by canoe.

In the Talmud, one of the repositories of the Jewish oral law, there are over 60 tractates of legal and other material. At the end of each tractate there is a short sentence that means essentially "We will return to you, Tractate So and So", meaning that we are done reading and studying that tractate for now, but we plan to read and study it again soon.

The feeling that is expressed in that Talmudic statement reflects the feeling that I have about Rainy River. I enjoy returning to it again and again in my mind, and every time I return, my memories of Rainy River comfort me and help me find peace.

ABOUT THE AUTHORS

Toby M. Gershfield was born in Winnipeg, Manitoba in 1933, and has lived in the United States since marrying her husband, the late Rabbi Edward M. Gershfield, in 1953. She holds a Bachelors degree from the University of Manitoba, and a Masters degree in Administration from Teachers College, Columbia University in the City of New York.

James N. Gershfield is Toby's son, and has a Bachelors degree in Computing Science from Columbia College in the City of New York and a Masters degree in Computer Engineering from the University of Michigan, Ann Arbor. After working as a software engineer for over 40 years, he changed his focus to writing, editing and publishing books by founding Scribal Scion Publishing LLC, the publisher of this book.

www.ingramcontent.com/pod-product-compliance
Lightning Source LLC
Chambersburg PA
CBHW070717130626
46553CB00005B/2029